Bits and Pieces

Start collecting bits and pieces to make the wonderful pictures in this book. You'll need paper and card, wool and felt, sequins and beads, foil, glitter and paints, sponge and fancy sweet wrappers. You can either make the pictures just the same as the ones in the book, or you can use the ideas to design your own. There are all sorts of exciting and unusual painting techniques for you to try out as well.

Acknowledgements

Designed by **Jane Warring**
Illustrations by **Lindy Norton**
Pictures made by **Karen Radford**
Photographs by **Peter Millard**
Created by **Thumbprint Books**

First published in hardback in 1995,
first published in paperback in 1995
by Hamlyn Children's Books
an imprint of Reed Children's Books
Michelin House, 81 Fulham Road
London SW3 6RB

Hardback ISBN 0600 584771
Paperback ISBN 0600 586162

Printed and bound in Belgium by Proost

Making Pictures
OUT OF THIS WORLD

Penny King and Clare Roundhill

SHERRARDSWOOD SCHOOL

LOCKLEYS WELWYN

Contents

HAMLYN

A Man in the Moon

Have you ever looked up at the night sky and seen the face of the man-in-the-moon looking back at you? Make your own picture of him from yellow crumpled crêpe paper. Give him a smiling mouth and a beady red eye.

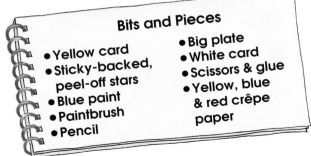

Bits and Pieces
- Yellow card
- Sticky-backed, peel-off stars
- Blue paint
- Paintbrush
- Pencil
- Big plate
- White card
- Scissors & glue
- Yellow, blue & red crêpe paper

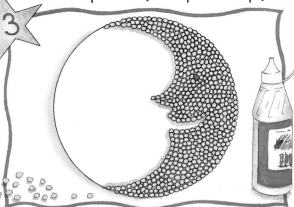

Stick peel-off stars all over the yellow card. Cover the card with blue paint (see paint tip).

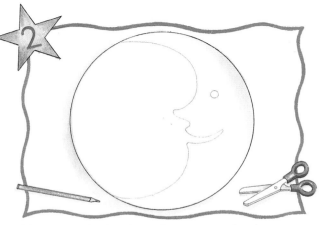

Use a plate to draw a circle on the white card. Cut it out. Draw a man-in-the-moon's face on it.

Glue crumpled balls of yellow crêpe paper on the man-in-the-moon's face. Add an eye.

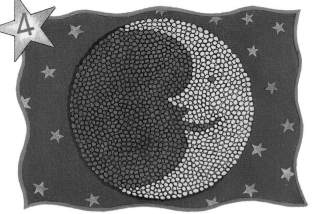

Stick blue crêpe paper balls over the rest of the moon. Glue it on to the starry sky.

7

A Glittering Galaxy

This startling picture with all its vibrant colours looks like a real map of the galaxy.

To make it glisten, sprinkle on glitter when the paint is wet. Glue on sequin stars.

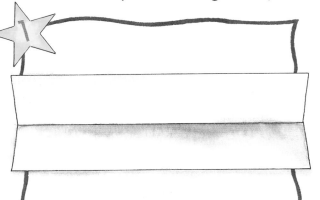

Fold the stiff paper in half lengthways. Press firmly along the fold. Open it out again.

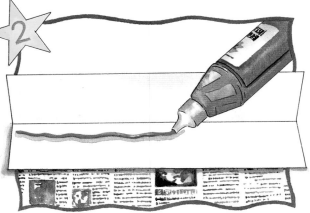

Squirt a squiggly line of red paint straight from the bottle along one side of the fold.

Bits and Pieces

- Long sheet of stiff white paper
- Red, yellow, blue & bright green paint in plastic bottles
- Newspaper
- Silver & gold glitter
- Pink and gold, sequin stars
- Glue

PAINT TIP
Smooth the paper gently from the fold outwards, towards the edges. This smudges the lines of paint together and produces a truly surprising effect.

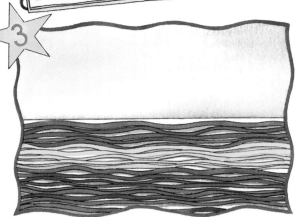

Squirt yellow paint next to the red, green next to the yellow and blue next to the green.

Fold the paper in half again. Press it gently on the top (see paint tip). Open up the paper.

9

An Awesome Alien

Have you ever wondered what creatures from outer space might look like? Do you think they have three heads and blue hair, or are they small, grey and very wrinkly? Paint a picture of your idea of an alien, using this sponging technique.

Bits and Pieces

- Yellow card
- Pencil
- Sponge
- Scissors
- Paints
- Paint palette
- Paintbrush
- Sequins
- Silver foil
- Glue
- String
- Shiny stars

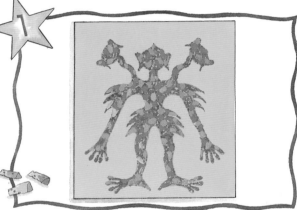

Draw the outline of an alien on the yellow card. Cover it with sponge prints (see paint tip).

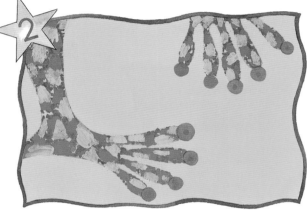

Dip your little finger in red paint. Use it to print splodgy toe and finger nails, like this.

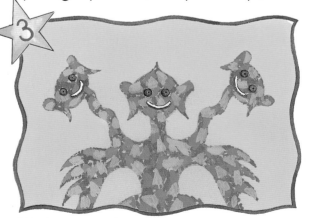

Stick on coloured sequin eyes. For the mouths, glue on short lengths of twisted silver foil.

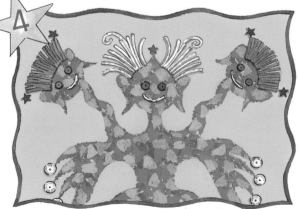

Stick on coloured string or twisted foil hair. Decorate the alien with stars, sequins and foil.

10

PAINT TIP

Cut a sponge into several shapes. Mix up different shades of green paint. Dip each sponge shape into one of the shades. Then print overlapping shapes inside the outline of the alien.

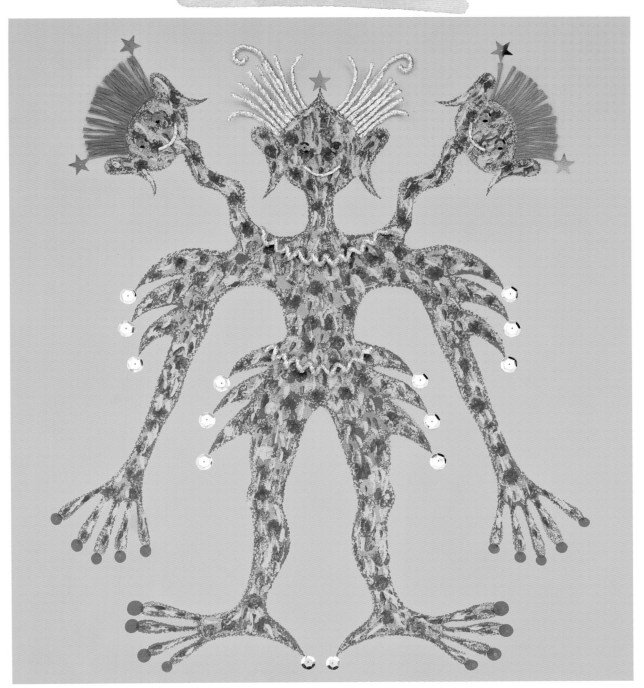

An Unusual UFO

Put together an amazing collage of a UFO taking off from a faraway planet.

Find pictures of machines in magazines to cut up for each part of the UFO.

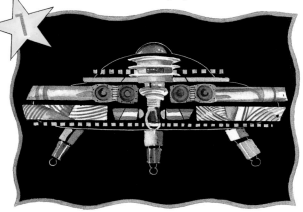

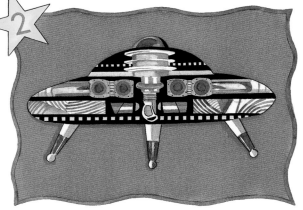

Draw a UFO on black paper with a crayon. Stick on silvery pictures cut from old magazines.

Carefully cut out the finished UFO shape. Then glue it on to the middle of the pink card.

PAINT TIP
To make the steam, dab some cotton wool into a pot of undiluted white paint. Then dab the paint in swirls on to the pink background card, below and around the UFO. Try to make the steam thicker along the bottom of the card and a little bit wispier as it rises.

Bits and Pieces

- Black paper
- White crayon
- Scissors & glue
- Shapes cut out of old magazines
- Pink card
- Cotton wool
- White paint
- Old saucer
- Shiny black paper

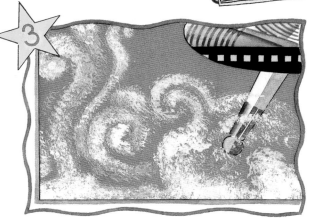

Add clouds of swirling steam (see paint tip). Practise first on a separate piece of paper.

Cut out strange aliens from shiny black paper. Glue them to the bottom of the picture.

13

Peculiar Planets

Use the magical technique of marbling to create this fantastic picture of some mysterious planets with their clouds of swirling gas. Add a couple of colourful stars made out of card, and roaring rockets with sweeping trails of glitter.

Bits and Pieces

- Marbling tray or washing up bowl
- Marbling ink in different colours
- Knitting needle or pencil
- White paper
- Scissors & glue
- Purple card
- Silver glitter
- Coloured card
- White spirit & rag

Put 2cm of water into the tray. Drip a few drops of each colour ink on to the water's surface.

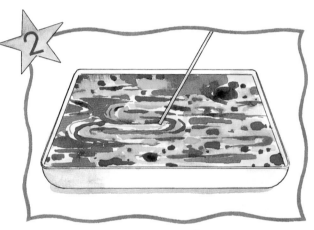

Mix the inks gently together with the knitting needle. Add more ink if you want stronger colours.

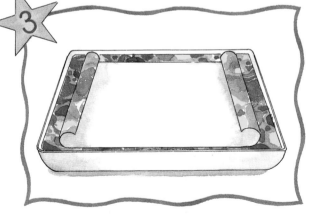

Put some white paper on top of the water. When the edges begin to curl, lift it off. Let it dry.

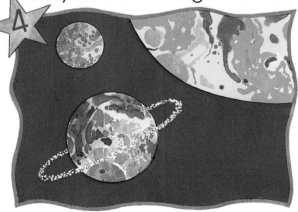

Cut planets out of the marbled paper. Glue them on to the purple card. Add glitter rings.

PAINT TIP
Marbling inks stain easily,
so it's best to work near
a sink. Wear old clothes and
cover the work surface.
Make sure you have some
white spirit and a rag on
hand to mop up any spills.

15

Cosmic Volcanoes

Make a red-hot landscape covered in cosmic craters and erupting volcanoes.

If you want, add rocks of sponge, painted orange and sprinkled with glitter.

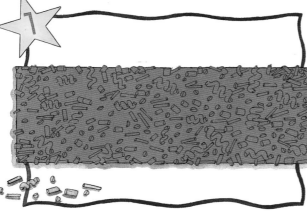

Spread glue over the orange card. Stick on dried pasta. Paint it orange (see paint tip).

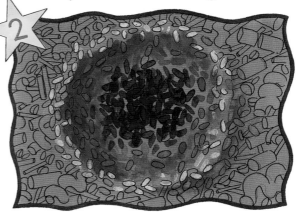

Make wells of rice on top of the pasta. Paint them purple and orange with yellow rims.

PAINT TIP

You may need a sponge as well as a brush to paint uneven surfaces. Make sure the paint is watery, so that it seeps into all the little cracks and crevices in the pasta.

To make volcanoes, cut the tops off plastic bottles. Glue on rice and then paint it purple.

Add tissue and tinsel flames to make the volcanoes fiery. Glue them on to the pasta base.

17

A Roaring Rocket

How about making this magnificent silver rocket roaring off into space with tissue flames shooting out of its engines? Decorate it with stripes and circles cut out of coloured paper. Add a big printed planet and lots of sparkling spirals.

Bits and Pieces
- Thin card
- Teacup
- Pencil & scissors
- Sticky tape
- Loo roll tube
- Silver foil
- Coloured paper
- Glue
- Black card
- Tissue paper
- Paints & rag
- Glitter

1 Cut out a card circle the size of a teacup. Snip it to the middle. Bend it into a cone and tape it.

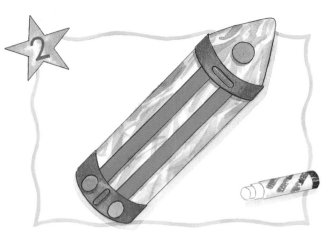

2 Tape the cone to a loo roll. Cover them both with silver foil and then glue on decorations.

3 Cover a big triangle of card with foil. Stick it on to the black card. Stick the rocket on top.

4 Glue tissue flames to the rocket. Add a planet (see paint tip), and spirals of glitter and glue.

Sunstorm

Make this hot and stormy sun with brilliant rays of light and heat bursting out.

Have fun flicking on fiery paint colours. Watch how they run and mix together.

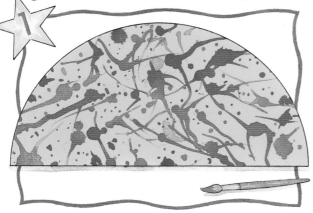

Cut a big semi-circle out of bright yellow card. Flick paint over it (see paint tip). Let it dry.

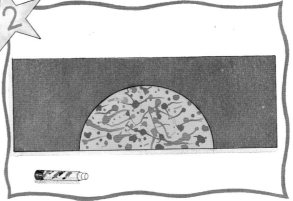

Glue the sun on to the blue card. Make sure the flat edge sits along the bottom, like this.

PAINT TIP
Put yellow paint into three wells of your palette. Add a little red to one and mix it. Add more red to the next, and still more to the third. Dip your brush into each colour in turn and flick it all over the yellow sun.

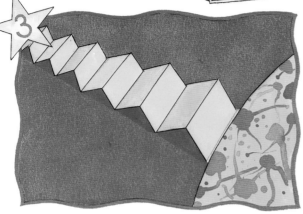

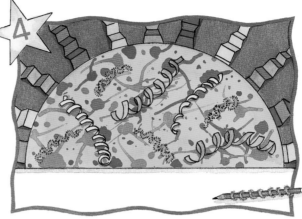

Fold up long, thin triangles of orange, yellow and red card. Glue them around the sun.

Curl lengths of paper ribbon and pipe-cleaners round a pencil. Glue them on the sun.

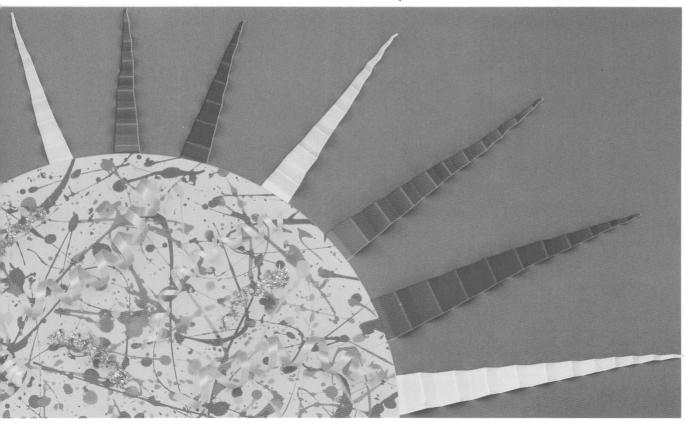

21

An Amazing Astronaut

The astronaut in this picture is all dressed up and ready for his walk on the moon. Decorate his space suit with all sorts of shiny bits and pieces. Then make a border of his footprints around the edge of the picture (see paint tip).

1 Cut the astronaut suit out of stiff yellow paper. Stick it on to the red card, as shown.

2 Glue on corrugated card boot soles, silver foil gloves and a painted pink card face.

3 Cut out the bottom of a foil pie tin. Cover the hole with cling film. Glue the tin over the face.

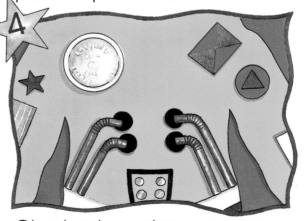

4 Glue badges, straws, paper, polystyrene and foil decorations on the space suit.

22

Cut a footprint shape from
corrugated card. Brush watery
black paint all over the bumpy
side of the card. Then press it
firmly on to the red card.
Print all the footprints going
in the same direction.

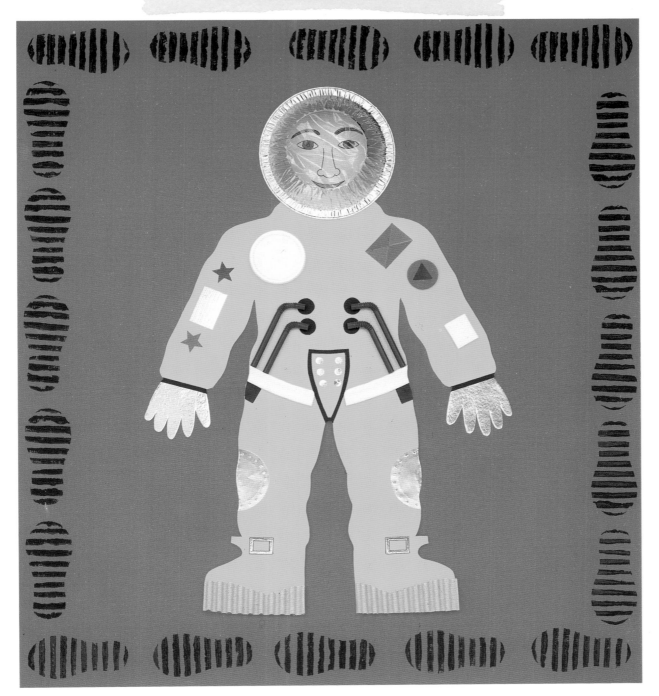

23

Shooting Stars

Create a spectacular night sky picture with sparkling stars shooting across it.

Make the stars different sizes and colours, covered with gold and silver glitter.

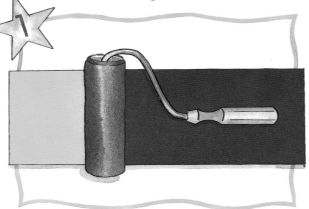

Cover a long piece of yellow card with a thick layer of floury dark blue paint (see paint tip).

While it is still wet, scratch stars out of the paint, using a knitting needle or a sharp pencil.

PAINT TIP
For the night sky, mix blue paint with enough flour to make it nice and thick. Use a sponge roller or a fat brush to spread the mixture evenly all over the yellow card.

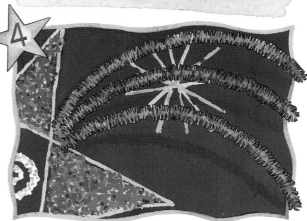

3 When the paint is dry, brush PVA glue over some of the stars. Sprinkle them with glitter.

4 Use glittery pipe-cleaners to make tails for the shooting stars. Stick them on with strong glue.

A Command Module

Make a dramatic picture of a command module, like this, about to plunge into the sea on its return from a trip to the moon. Paint the parachutes, which slow down its flight, with bold, colourful stripes, and attach them with shiny foil strips.

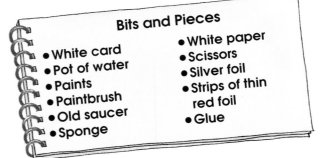

Bits and Pieces

- White card
- Pot of water
- Paints
- Paintbrush
- Old saucer
- Sponge
- White paper
- Scissors
- Silver foil
- Strips of thin red foil
- Glue

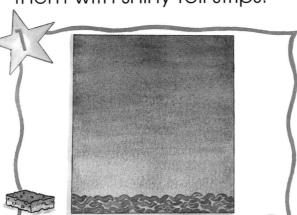

1. Paint a streaky blue sky and swirly, frothy waves on the white card (see paint tip).

2. Cut out a paper module. Glue on silver foil, like this. Cut strips of foil for the parachute strings.

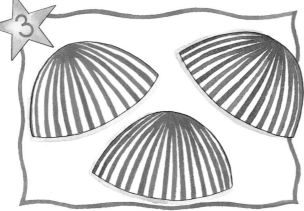

3. Cut three parachute shapes from white paper. Paint red, blue or green stripes on them.

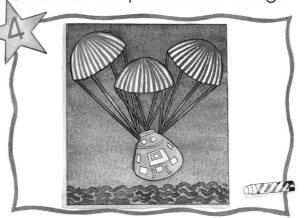

4. Stick the module and the foil strips on the sky, and then the three parachutes, as shown.

26

PAINT TIP
Paint a pale blue sky on the white card. Blend streaks of blue on top with a damp sponge. Make the streaks darker blue at the top and paler nearer the bottom. Paint on waves with a brush.

27

Crazy Control Deck

This crazy control deck with all its knobs and buttons makes a brilliant picture. You don't have to make it exactly as it is here. Create your own using all sorts of odds and ends. Design your own special screen with a view of outer space.

Bits and Pieces

- Black, silver & white card
- Scissors & glue
- Candle & corks
- Paints & brush
- Silver glitter
- Plastic cartons
- Silver & gold foil
- Boxes & paper
- Drinking straws
- Paper fasteners
- Yogurt pots

Cut out a silver card TV screen. Paint an outer space view (see paint tip). Glue it on the screen.

Stick the screen on to the black card. Glue boxes covered with shiny paper squares next to it.

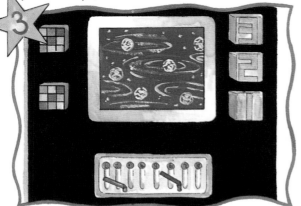

Stick down three numbers and cover them with see-through lids. Make a plastic fuel gauge.

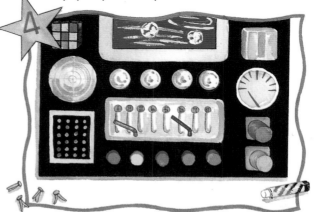

Glue on small yogurt pot and painted cork knobs, foil dials and paper fastener controls.

PAINT TIP
Draw spirals on white paper
with the end of a white
candle. Brush blue paint
over the paper. Let it dry.
Print on planets using a cork
and white paint. Add blobs
of glue and silver glitter.